THE SINKING ROAD

Paul Batchelor was born in Northumberland in 1977. In 2003 he received an Eric Gregory Award from the Society of Authors, and in 2004 he was given the Andrew Waterhouse Award by New Writing North. In 2005 he was a winner of the Poetry Business Prize; his pamphlet *To Photograph a Snow Crystal* was published by Smith/Doorstop in 2006. He is editing a collection of critical essays on Barry MacSweeney, to be published by Newcastle University and Bloodaxe Books.

PAUL BATCHELOR

THE SINKING ROAD

BLOODAXE BOOKS

ISBN: 978 1 85224 807 9

First published 2008 by
Bloodaxe Books Ltd,
Highgreen,
Tarset,
Northumberland NE48 1RP.

www.bloodaxebooks.com
For further information about Bloodaxe titles
please visit our website or write to
the above address for a catalogue.

Bloodaxe Books Ltd acknowledges
the financial assistance of
Arts Council England, North East.

Cover design: Neil Astley & Pamela Robertson-Pearce.

Printed in Great Britain by
Bell & Bain Limited, Glasgow, Scotland.

i.m. Oz

The boundaries of the senses are not often clearly
realised. The Infra and the Ultra are fields easily
forgotten. Out of hearing stays unthought-of; out
of sight is out of mind. And yet, how haunted we
all are.

DAVID GASCOYNE

ACKNOWLEDGEMENTS

Acknowledgements are due to the editors of the following publications, in which some of these poems first appeared: *Modern Poetry in Translation*, *The North*, *Poetry Ireland Review*, *Poetry London*, *Poetry Review*, *Poetry Wales*, *Shearsman*, *Stand*, *Stride*, *The Times Literary Supplement*, *Tower Poetry Review* and *The Wolf*.

Some of these poems appeared in two pamphlets, *Fighting in the Captain's Tower*, written with J.P. Nosbaum (Hawthorn, 2002), and *To Photograph a Snow Crystal* (Smith/Doorstop, 2006).

'Butterwell' was commissioned by Culture North East and New Writing North. I am grateful to the Society of Authors, the Blue Mountain Centre and New Writing North for help and support.

I would like to thank my brother Gav, Sasha Dugdale, Jeff Nosbaum, Sean O'Brien and Denise Riley. Love and thanks to Rachael Ogden.

CONTENTS

According to Culpeper

Whose tender demand
        makes the hawthorn bend
                & sunlight concede

a sweet inhaling
        finer than honey,
                a narcotic soft

as babies' breath
        & summary justice
                according to Culpeper

for headaches, breathlessness,
        insomnia & all
                manner of affections of the heart?

To Photograph a Kingfisher

A bracket exposure.
At Limerick market
            your grandfather's grandfather
is selling a kingfisher.
            A gypsy in love
with long distances, he
            is travelling light:
a basket of eggs,
            the names of his women;
a song for each one
            is easily carried.

Previsualise.
Turning out a bag
            of scraps & clippings,
feeling the baby
            kick inside her,
your grandfather's mother
            is making a hooky mat
in the likeness of a kingfisher.
            A parallax:
her husband is planning
            to take up with a fancy woman.

Widen the aperture.
Your grandfather is finding
            the body of a kingfisher
in a glim of ice.
            He cradles the crush
of orange & blue
            as he'll nurse his daughter
through rheumatic fever,
            carrying her out
like a basket of eggs
            when the doctor won't come.

Develop, agitate.
Like a rumour of winter
            in living colour,
there is the kingfisher
            caught in the frame:
a snapshot memento,
            a lock of red hair
easily carried
            easily held
between finger & thumb
            as if for safe keeping.

Butterwell

Nightdriving. Going to pick dad up from work.
Singing *Dance to Your Daddy* as the road unwinds,
a cine-film pitted with potholes. Cat's-eyes.
An allotment flae-craa sucking its fangs
by the stob where they hanged the last Ranter.
Where Jesus met the woman with five husbands.
Where the tigers turn to butter. Where they bury
men alive, black torchlight on the livid faces,
Netherton to Widdrington,
Widdrington to Seaton Burn.
Sedimental generations eking & hawking,
cavilling in Jolson monochrome. Butterwell.
A double scoop of Peroni's ice cream, the finest in Ashington
and the world. And the recipe gone: snow melt
from the hills of Butterwell. 'Somebody wants
to make the guy an offer really: patent it, they'll make a mint.'
A housing estate rechristened by council officials
in the wake of a scathing ITV documentary.
Our childhood word for cabbage whites: *butterlowie*.
Butterwell. Asking mam to tell us again
how the road was sinking because it was built
over the mine where granddad was buried alive
so often they nicknamed him *Jonah*. Driving on
past the watchtower in St Mary's churchyard, built
in 1830 to deter body snatchers from Makemland;
where I saw Aidan & Cuthbert knock the dirt off their boots;
where I saw slag heaps rise like smouldering hills of buttermilk;
where I saw Barabbas scabs
and selected representatives of the Tory party
in smurf-blue boiler suits & white hard hats
with red tape surveyors creep at night
to snatch our milk and poison every well. Butterwell.
The warning sign on the gate to the site.
The whistle at lowse, the wire fence, the floodlit watchtower.
The full moon poaching itself in the clouds.
Mam changing sides, winding the seat with a sheet,
while we press our noses to the glass & squeak
a cross in the mist to ward off the vampire

who is sliding up to the car on silent Nosferatu-rails;
who is climbing into the car, his donkey jacket heavy
with the odour of the mine (old earth freshly turned:
a smell that sticks to you, dogged as a lesson,
dogged as a lesson you wish you'd never learned);
who plants a kiss on mam's cheek & leaves a bruise.
And my brother & I nodding our pumpkin heads
and grinning our pumpkin grins.
And him reaching behind his seat
and grabbing our knees, his hand swinging like a shovel.

Tributes

Honesty

It was a 70s thing, a fad that every housewife kept
for show, the aspidistra of the working classes.
She let me dust the petals while she slept off her migraine.
Judas Money. I held my breath and brushed drab kisses
across each brittle window; never once popped
my finger through the tempting membrane. Honesty.
You think you've seen the last of it, then it ghosts
an old folk's home, or the dayroom of a slated hospital.
Lunaria Rediviva. Paper Moons. I find a spray
done up with peacock feathers in an Alston B&B
and hold my breath again. It seems to stand
for the little she aspired to; the less she was allowed;
for all the mindless tasks she found to keep me occupied.
Petal after petal gives between my thumb and forefinger.

Amaryllis Johnsonii

Amaryllis Johnsonii. A floral tribute
in memory of the Christmas you came down
with a stomach bug you thought was cancer.
St Joseph Lilies. Patron Saint of fathers.
All night, delirious, your secret fear
was bound up with their smell: a reesty savour;
the horse-stale tang of vase water gone over;
a reek that even now makes you recoil.
Come down again with promises to love
us all more fiercely. Don't wait until
St Joseph, Patron Saint of working men,
demands you ask yourself *What do I have
that answers this bouquet?* Breathe deep: the smell
will bring it back, like something on the turn.

Heartwood

I'm thinking of MacLeary's yew: the way
sapwood is subtle, apt, but must be lined
with heartwood to give it a backbone;
the way an arrow must spin in flight to stay
true; the way the fletches have to be aligned
just so; the way a longbow is drawn
to the ear, not the chest. Let's take the rest
(nocks, tillering, bracing height) on trust
or, better, turn it over: argue either side
and tomorrow, brother, not to harm
a living thing, make a bow so fine
it cannot tolerate an unschooled draw;
so femmor it disintegrates when, taking aim,
I loose an imaginary arrow.

Secret Papers

Something has splayed
the oak trunk in a dozen knotted tongues.

Nobody heard
the sound it made: would its song,

pure air and fire,
have split the ear?

Or might a tree
slip from its bark

quietly
as a girl steps from her clothes

to stand, stripped to the skin,
secret papers burnt?

Everything conspired.
A singling-out occurred.

Tree Climbing

Grasp this: it doesn't matter if the rasp
of bark to palm is second nature or
if this is your first time, there are

no experts: ash or oak, the look of bole
or canopy means nothing till you throw
yourself off balance, wrap

your feet around the branch you hold
and from that new perspective see
how the world hangs: head over heels

it all floods back to a heart
that won't forget vertigo's bloodrush
nor come down when they call.

Blodeuwedd

Damned if I'm writing this
for Jenny Houlet
    since she took to rousing me
at ungodly hours
    with her querulous call
to give my remembrances
    of the time she clocked me
asleep at the wheel
    then gave me the count of three
before we flew off the road
    to take a last-ditch look
at her heart shaped face
    and broad, white brow;
to recognise how
    she lit by my bed;
how she sat,
    dimples in her jaws,
till I opened my eyes:
    as if I'd applaud
the wings' silence or
    the grace with which
(on the count of three)
    they lifted her clear.

Artemis

Drunk, I lie face
down on the grass

to watch the moon
with the nape of my neck

as you'd watch a girl move
through a crowded room

for so
long that when you try to say hello

you find your tongue
has lost its cunning

like the peeping tom who broke
a tell-tale rose's back

or the lock
that swallowed its key

or the riverbed stone
(smooth as the nape of your neck)

that men in drink say fell
in love with the moon.

Pygmalion's Prayer to Venus

Once it was enough, more than enough,
to have your likeness carved in cedar; to kiss
your belly: cedar-gold; your shoulder: cedar-sweet.
Clear-eyed & kind, hear what I cannot say.

This careful likeness carved in cedar by
my journeyman hand looks well, but never well enough.
Clear-eyed & kind, hear all I dare not say:
your sympathetic magic knows

my journeyman heart too well, or well enough;
hear this sinner's prayer for flesh & blood.
Your sympathetic magic knows
I only ever worshipped you.

Grant my idiot wish for flesh & blood
and that will be enough, more than enough,
for one who only ever worshipped you,
your belly: cedar-gold; your shoulder: cedar-sweet...

Gilgamesh Rebukes Ishtar

tell me one • counting your lovers • one you serve truly
what of Tamuzzi • how you love him • dragging him down
already bored • calling nine demons • nine women in Uruk
beating their brows • pet [lorikeet] • keening yet
wings torn out • how you love him • hearing him grieve
fourteen finding • mountain lion • cedar grove
misused strength • fluent weaponry • digging a grave
what of your lust • battle-scarred stallion • cursing the beast
tasting the bit • whip and spur • galloping always
bereft of sense • how you love him • queenly bequest
piss in his waterhole • goddess Silili • endless disgrace
what of your shepherd • tender hand • baking biscuits
newborn lamb • [buckling/bending] • making him butcher
knuckled wolf • how you love him • dutiful son
digging a trench • dogs he trained • trailing his scent
last Ishullanu • hungry eye • figs and dates
farmer's gifts • [tilth/mulch] • gracing your table
licked teeth • breath in his ear • 'Husbandman Ishullanu
hold out your hand • test how wet • give me your cock'
and he fearful • 'Shall I fare • scraps and slop
shame and dishonour • Ishtar's fare • sow on her litter
me with a home • out in the wind' • quickly broken
trusted lovetricks • so you serve him • making him a toad
poisoning his garden • nothing grows • were I your man
will you deny it • act in kind • tell me the reason
were I your sweet man • counting your lovers • my fate will be different

The Anatomy Lesson

I

Towards the end, when it was obvious,
the couple we called George & Martha asked for water:
'*Tap* water, mind: we won't be paying for it!'
We cackled into our antipasto, then opted for the Châteauneuf-du-Pape,
pretending not to watch them bicker, send food back,
dispute the bill or pocket an extra after-dinner mint.
'They come here every week to have that argument...'
'And then go home and fuck like maniacs.'

Back home, you necked the Nurofen:
'Forget it... look, I'm *okay*... put the kettle on...'
'But is it broken?'
                    '*No*... just sore.'
                                        'But still...'
Don't read too much into the way I slammed the taxi door
and nearly broke your thumb. I'd had too much to drink.
I tipped until the taxi driver shook his head.

II

How glad I was you let me watch you paint.
That birthmark on your ankle, the stretch-mark
tigering your arse... 'Jesus!'
                          'That's nothing,' you replied
and gave me an old-fashioned look: 'Just my final submission:
a "creative response" to *The Anatomy Lesson*.'
I nearly said that Dr Tulp looked like an artist poised
before a canvas, but got back to...(what was it, *Life Studies?*)
and let the moment pass.

You go to get cleaned up. I rub some life into my hands.
Since your studio is closed to me now
surely as it ever was, you'll never know
how glad I am I pocketed the key. Shall I steal
inside again to see your drying colours; touch
those skins peeled from the air?

III

Even decked-out in silver rings, your hands were peasant hands:
'Shtetl hands,' you called them. I see them swim my creamy belly.
I see them give me five or six matronly strokes.
I hear your mother tell you, 'Fold your arms, girl.'
I watch you skin a hare or stretch a canvas. I watch you sculpt
a clay clod in my likeness, lop my head clean off then place it
very gently in the kiln. It was the summer of slopped
shopping bags, abandoned dishes of ratatouille,
sugar-paper eyelids, skin like chilled honey and waspish fingers.
It was the summer you turned your studio upside down
looking for the ring your father gave you.
I stole it. Look: I've put it in my mouth again
thinking how I'd suck your fingers: here it is.
So: how am I to be punished?

IV

Assuming the position, I did the best I could.
'Don't fucking *move!*' Stripped bare,
my attitudinising put to service, I was Aris Kindt,
'The main attraction,' you assured me. Hold it there:
you painting me while I re-jig a poem in my head,
telling my heart (whatever I meant by heart) to listen
to its heart; telling my soul to look into its soul
(whatever I meant by soul). I didn't move.

A get-together three months on. 'I just thought it'd be nice,
as friends...' I sip my frappuccino in cold blood
and, apropos of nothing, raise
a glass to you for never looking back.
Before the talk resumes, I note
the girl who wipes the table has your ankles.

V

I draw it out, the spliff you left me, and imagine
artful hands arranging Rizlas, tamping the tobacco;
your tradesman's patter; you the chin-to-chest apothecary
with the storehouse of pot stories. I take a pull
and then another, and then lie back to watch you float
across the floor, my waitress for the evening.
In my dream restaurant you've yet to hear
my jokes, my stories, my so many words. I've yet to tell
'Enough white lies to ice a wedding cake...'
George & Martha storm out. We share a tight-lipped smile
at their promise never to come back. Soon, I'll
ask your name, when you'll be finishing. Behind the bar,
the sign we'll laugh at: *No Happy Hour in December.*
The wine arrives, but if I drink it I wake up.

VI

Don't let another summer bleed into the beech leaves.
Don't wait for frost, impeccable, to feather every blade of grass.
Your car is waiting, waiting. I can see
seat covers fading by degrees; can hear
the sycamore weep honeydew upon it.
If you come back I'll charm an alleycat to swim
about your ankles in a welcome; you'll feel a warm
breeze nuzzle at your back.

Even now, in enormous numbers, late leaves are flying.
The roads unwind from your door.
In the arbour, I close my eyes and see
you bend, dab paint, then pause,
a doctor poised to test a sore-point,
and step back into sunlight, years ago.

To Photograph a Snow Crystal

                    Hokkaido, '54.
Ukichiro Nakaya
                    coaxes a crystal
into life on a rabbit hair
                    in an unlikely menagerie
of stellar dendrites,
                    double stars,
sectored plates,
                    crystal twins,
clusters, bullets
                    & chandeliers.
The fickle, sixfold
                    symmetry of snowflakes.
The fourteen identified
                    varieties of ice.
Why do complex patterns
                    arise spontaneously
in simple physical
                    systems? Trust me, love,
to make heavy weather
                    of first principles.
What might I make
                    of these arabesques:
facets & lattices,
                    glyphs & ciphers,
shapes with which
                    you decorate your poems?

The Permafrost: an A–Z

The Permafrost is quietly spoken, disliking sudden noise or sudden gesture. Despite this, it is remarkably hospitable, enjoying long hours of easy talk, during which one might detect its eagerness to agree.

The Permafrost is able to convince, but rarely to persuade. The uninitiated see nothing but scrubland, and complain of 'being cold'. By such signs are they to be identified.

The Permafrost must never be referred to as *tundra*.

The Permafrost sounds like an ailing synthesiser. It is 1982 at the best of times. 'They used to grow grapes here,' the natives boast. How little must have been promised these people; how little they must feel they are owed: they do not even refer to their ancestors as 'we'.

The Permafrost is noted for an absence of birdsong: a policy of the leisure & tourism industry.

The Permafrost is surrounded by hills and small mountains. Many resemble the sleeping forms of females. A policy of the leisure & tourism industry.

The Permafrost is densely populated, despite its reputation. Colonies are rare, but not unknown. Usually, an individual will acquire a smallholding with the intention of using it as a holiday home or retreat. All will tell you they are passing through. More and more residents are choosing to raise families there.

The Permafrost can draw surprising admissions from some residents, who liken it to the process of hypnosis. You are encouraged to keep a record of your stay.

The Permafrost is a voluntary organisation, run by dedicated individuals who have taken time out of their busy schedules. It takes no responsibility for belongings including articles of clothing that are lost or damaged during your stay. It does not supply consumables.

The Permafrost handles unpredictably in confined spaces and is capable of elaborate structures when base restrictions are applied. It can be likened to a panic room and the anxiety induced by knowing such a place exists.

The Permafrost is habitually frugal, but will occasionally disarm with a show of generosity, as in the provision of blotting paper or funeral meats. Nothing is grudged because nothing is given: complimentary gifts are covered by your initial payment.

The Permafrost is carpeted throughout with a fully up-to-date kitchen and self-cleaning oven. Relax in a peaceful environment free from distractions. A curfew is currently in operation, exact times to be announced.

Triage

Assuming *noblesse oblige*.
Assuming responsibility. Assuming
disciplined dissent to desperate
measures, to boulevards of broken bones.
Laying your watch face down the way
an angler waits for silly fish to wash
your hands each time the phone
rings in the empty room to which
a rucksack opens like a mouth
that tells the concierge to get
some sleep. A landmine waiting.
A child: maimed, sent out begging.
A briefcase closing like a wound.
r u ok
Laying down the receiver as
you would a tired child & when
the room swims with the smell of soap & fine
Egyptian cotton closing your eyes. Not crying.
Hearing a train scrape home on time to ask
if soldiers joke about a smell
like rosewater. Allowing
laundered sheets to swaddle you. Allowing
the barber to sweep about your feet & slip
the conversation into neutral till
the world stands by to watch
a child play dead/ roll over/ lift
her paw. Only so much you can do.
Death comes in colours, who
can name them? Helicopters waltzing
heartbeats that provide us with
important information. After the massacre, easing
their consciences with smaller deaths.
Looking like rain. Laughing.

Lebiyska Mova

He tells of *Kobzari*
    making their rounds
  at fairs & markets:
    blind street singers
    keepers of a secret history
      the struggle
        for the Black Sea steppe
        Cossack rebellions
          fallen heroes
      the cruelty of the Turk

Of impeccably played bandura
    of Fedir the Cold One
   sleeping in a ditch,
  Fedir whose voice
     was a jet of blood with grief in it
    proclaiming the truth
      in *lebiyska mova*
      a gospel in tomorrow's language

Of a village where the butcher starves
  the shoemaker goes barefoot
  and someone saws a bed in half
    to make a bed

Died, all, in the terror

In a Mission
in Colonia Esperança
    he composes
  a final *dumy*
    explaining
      to the anthropologist
      with his reel-to-reel
    that when the pitch is bent
   and sharp or flat notes
     slip into the scale
   it is called
     dodavaty zhaloshchiv:
  'adding the sorrow'

Keening

The quality of keening is not narrow.
It ranges freely: back roads, low roads,
a violin heard from a window at night,
a silken rubbing, a tune you can't place,
a fellside lapwing signalling in slate grey rain:
all these betoken keening. It travels incognito
as lyric, or as perfume from a dress;
passes customs unfazed; is taken as currency
everywhere, ache bearing witness to ache.
Keening puts words in hungry mouths,
gives tongue without language, longing without hope.
With keening no man's hand is strong,
no heart true. It mars the wild
and we who were not wild enough are marred
equally. Truly your riches are worthless;
your poverty yet shall be rendered more bitter
with keening, who has no tears. Let blood be drawn
and let the dog be driven far from the hearth
before keening shares tears: beholden to no one
it suffers all woes that none may evade it.

Tristia

I

My friend, until you have been cursed
to wander, kinless, foreign lands where range
barbarians so foul the farmer goes
with a machete strung across his back
simply to milk his kine, you cannot know
time's secret ministries: how it can crawl
like a disease that steals
so sly upon a man he barely feels
its subtle victories; or like an army
marching at half speed. It's true: I have bogged down
in this forgotten outpost. Do not upbraid
narrowness of theme: I never wrote
to better purpose than when I implore
Augustus to be merciful.

II

I have bogged down here: a spit of land, a fistula
in the oxter of an Empire I once served.
In winter, the ocean freezes. Brigands
drive chariots over the ice, terrorise
farmers, raze the homesteads. Women
and livestock are seized while men are lashed
to stakes, compelled to watch their crops destroyed.
Leander would have found apt use
for such a frozen waste: he would have walked
the Hellespont's vault of glass, but those old
tales are not told here. Confined to bed,
I draft my epitaph: *Time that mocks*
bright blades with rust makes soft the bones
of he that lies here: Naso, who died for love.

III

Tristis lupus. I fall asleep among the men
and hear the voice of Erisycthon carry
over the trembling water. Hear him hawk
his trembling daughter, watch him cadge
a plate of food. Hear him howl
as wolves, grown fearful, leave off hunting
to watch each other starve. I need
no oread to tell me exile is
a parable of my oppressor's anger:
when I imagined Scythia,
the permafrost where Hunger
scavenges, I knew how finely calibrated
a deadfall I had found. Fate licked her teeth.
I woke among the keening wolves.

IV

The gods flee to the stars where they become
daft stories poets use
to show their mastery of form;
an exercise in rhyme.

Perhaps a corner yet remains in Rome
that holds in reverence the name
of one who versed with bite:
wherever poets meet

let the best chair stand empty;
let them remember
Naso, who would not stoop to wring
old metre from a heathen tongue,

who shamed the gods with his inventions
and found men less forgiving.

V

My favourites? Those who shamed the gods.
My favourite theme? Divine punishment
carried over, as when, naked at the window,
Arachne translates Jove's assembled rapes
enraptured by her own accomplishment.
A tapestry like that will make her name.
Poor girl. Let's watch until she disappears:
it won't take long (though longer than you'd think),
Minerva jealoused her the day she was born.
Close by, a well trimmed taper sobs
over a rack of shuttles and pins. I note
the bunched back; the way she shows
an almost human eagerness to clinch
her theme; the dwindling spinnerets...

VI

I watch you wave and when you disappear
become a house where nobody lives,
an old façade decayed, a pillow bereft
of the smell of your hair. A stranger asks
but nobody can place who lived in that
boarded-up ruin children say is haunted,
where manuscripts lie strewn about the floor;
where lemon trees have overrun the orchard;
where, in the quartered fields, stogged wheat
reeks like a byre and rape holds sway.
You wave your arms and crows
scatter like crows. And that's the pose
in which I've held you (waiting, open armed)
for seven years. And I'm still here.

The Honest Sailor

You've heard the like, you've heard
about the honest sailor trapped
aboard the drunken ship. In this scenario
the captain, having nailed
a false log to the table, falls asleep
letting the crew continue its slow
drift into the deep straits where
far wide, our man's mind moves
as water moves: his one idea
to lie with her by simple shells (he's tried
before but, though the wind was North,
the ocean didn't want him, spat
him out & wiped its mouth).
She was the star he might have steered by,
her lovemaking: a flame on oil;
her laughter: soft as rain on cobblestone
laving his rough edges –
but he was busy with his maps & charts,
his wanderer's tale took a turn from one
abysmal shipwreck to the next
and now she's gone, gone, gone
forever while he watches small fry rise
to kiss the water surface, sip
the ordinary air, hoping
for a long legged fly but making do
with cheap tricks, feathery stuff...
He's sure one day he'll do it: sail away,
never seen again. You've heard the like.

Conurbation

The day you left they pulled your picture from its frame and tore
the posters from your walls: immaculate, monastic,
boasting no trace that you were ever there, didn't that blank
plaster prove the house had never loved you? Scrub the floor.

Boil the sheets. One day you'll feel the city's dirt
bed down beneath your fingernails; you'll tilt the blinds,
look out over council flats and office blocks,
see lamps appear in living rooms like riding lights

and lose your fear of kitchens in which eggs and bacon
squabble in the pan, where a TV waits on standby in each room,
where children still fall silent at the slam of a door,
where, when a cigarette clears a throat, it passes for conversation.

You'll wonder how you stood it for so long: a house
that never learned how to exhale. You'll close the window, turn
back to the bed as one by one the panes fill up with snow,
and that's where you'll be hiding when you get called home.

Findings

I

He settles in the burn
till snow melt smoothes his young face younger still.
I would recall
all the lost places of his life & find them new again,
the images to which he will return:
a fossil of two fern leaves, which he found & gave to me;
a nest
of baby weasels, bald & reptilian.

He says *We'd best work fast*,
and drops his handkerchief into the nest:
the cauldron seethes: claws & teeth
needle the handkerchief.
When they're attached, he lifts a clutch
of weasels up for me to see.

II

My body will blacken and turn into coal. A Johnny Cash *basso profundo*
echoes around the house-end: Dark as a Dungeon, Chicken Road.
Jimmie Rodgers, Tennessee Ernie Ford.
Trouble In Mind, Come Back to Sorrento.
An old song travels lightly. What about a garage full
of dead TV sets, vacuum cleaners, knick-knacks
that never quite took off? The cartridge player & the Betamax
to which he remained faithful.

What about a shadow on the lung? A blockage. An obstruction
found by chance. A routine check-up. Tests. Endoscopies,
appointments, cancellations, new appointments, consultations...
The doctors' names grow nearly reassuring.
A papery handshake from a specialist.
An x-ray of two fern leaves on the screen.

III

I wheel him through the hospice, trailing the pibroch.
In the foyer, a band plays fiddle, small pipes & a bodhrán;
when they strike up *Eileen Aroon*
he sings *Eilonóir a Rúin*. Gaelic:
a language no one living has heard him speak.
His body is womanish;
the belly: soft; the pectorals: slack flesh.
It's time to take him back.

I duck out of the room to let
the nurse lay him out. When I return
he's large as life, decorated
with bedsores, bruises & gauze: a boxer propped
waiting for the coach to slip him the gumshield, swab the sweat
and shove him stumbling back into the ring.

IV

A sentence handed down from 1932
opens on to your last hours.
Still in the private room they granted you,
I hear your breathing rise
from some unfathomable depth
as I put in order
your father's last words
before he upped & left:

Down the pit they can use
lads your age: they set you on
as trappers on the barrow-way.
I close my eyes
and hear, a mile below my feet, wind issuing
through a hundred long-abandoned doors.

V

In '36
I got a job at Kielder forest, snedding trees.
There was this burn where I would go to wash at lowse,
just like a fox...
I laugh: a fox?
But when I picture you, pearls snaking from your mouth & nose,
I see, behind the river's mirror, waiting for the hunt to lose
his trail, a fox –

till you correct me: when a fox is full of lice
he settles in a burn, his snout above the water,
a twig between his teeth. I have no
idea if this is true. The lice
swarm over him & gather
on the twig. When it is full, he lets it go: so.

Snow Melt

winter pasture,
clotted rain,
snow first-footing
the new year

*

bridled with ice
the beck is down:
it has been snowing
it will snow

*

threading moor
and skyline together,
a red threat of fox
flagging the field

stand silently & go

*

a world spins
wintering
under each
eyelid

*

knuckled feet
gather in,
blade of the spine
an upturned boat

*

this is a man:
body of Christ
life in his teeth
snow in his mouth

stand silently & go

*

melt & make
no noise: this life,
this crucible
of accidents

*

is ice what happens
when water forgets
how to be anything
else?

*

snow melt over-
fills the burn,
stots off stone,
tells it clean

stand silently & go

48

The Butcher's Daughter

I *Riesenbeck, autumn, 1946*

From the churchyard wall, you sketch the market square.
Some locals pass: you nod, they look away.

Now some of your lot.
Cadging a cigarette,

you draw a cartoon Hitler on the gatepost:
an angry egg with a toothbrush moustache.

The men *Sieg Heil*, you prop
a helmet on top

and then she's running at you: Mia Eilers,
the butcher's daughter, nine years old:

You didn't know him: Herr Hitler: ein Mann des Volkes!
Weißt du noch, wie arm wir damals waren?

Don't you know what the country
used to be like!
                    A crowd collects;

Geordie Hilloughby's in fits:
Fraternising with the enemy, Bill?

Or have you picked a fight?
Good to see you've picked your size...

And then she's gone.
The crowd resumes its stations.

You find a rag and start to rub the gatepost clean.

II *Itzehoe, summer, 1946*

Two hundred prisoners, two dozen guards
and a problem with the train. The station simmers.

Your guard dog pants and pants and pants and gulps.
Geordie makes the best of it,

thumb hooked in the strap of his Sten,
exchanging packets of cigarettes

for watches and wedding rings;
telling the ones who will not trade

they're headed for a concentration camp.
The rumour starts to take,

and now a prisoner spits a gob of phlegm
in Geordie's face.

Sunlight swarms
as Geordie swings the metal stock.

The fourth
or fifth blow splits the prisoner's scalp.

III *Riesenbeck, autumn, 1946*

A bible, a washstand and a bed.
A photograph: two brothers grin

in their new uniforms. You tear
the mattress open, flip it in the air

and drag the washstand from the wall:
there's Geordie's wallet, still full

of useless money. What to do now?
Where to say you found it?

Herr Eilers stops you at the door:
Mia ist kein Dieb.

Es Muß Hans sein.
                    So Hans is summoned:
he gazes at the mess in Mia's room.

He's simple; you can see that now.
Unbuckling his belt, the butcher twists

his mouth as at a bitter taste.

IV *Lingen, Christmas Day, 1946*

Over bottles of Kölsch you trade stories, you
and the Captain who swears he knows you from Sandhurst.

Whoever he is, he's had a good war:
If you ever need a favour doing, Bill...

You talk of Mia: her family starving; you smuggling
food from the cookhouse:

brisket, butter, tins of fruit...
How you're sure she didn't take the wallet.

How Hans would not admit he'd stolen it
and how they flogged him.

How it made you think of Dresden;
the children begging for *Schokolade*

or cigarettes to trade for food;
and the burnt-out tank and the soup

they hosed out of it.
And when you ask, he signs a transport permit

that sends you back
to Riesenbeck.

V *Riesenbeck, New Year's Day, 1947*

Tuberkulose
Herr Eilers says,

handing you a sugar-pig gumdrop
and an ebony cigarette holder:

Sie bat uns: 'Wenn der Bill kommt,
gib ihm bitte diese Sachen.'

The churchyard unfamiliar in the snow,
you walk to Mia's grave.

Straight off, I recognised the cigarette holder:
belonged to Geordie, didn't it.

Seen him get it for a packet of tabs
on the platform at Itzehoe. Well. After that

I got demobbed, came home, picked up my service medals
and gave them to next door's bairn:

'Here's some medals for you to play with!'
They should have given me the Iron Cross.

I could never get away with the cigarette holder
but I kept it anyway, up on the pantry shelf,

and it stayed there fifty year. One day I noticed
it'd gone. But keep that to yourself, you hear?

SUIBNE CHANGED

Suibne Goes to War with the Hag of the Mill

A dream of war: you spare
my life so I become
    your slave. For seven years I play
the tailor's boy, contriving scraps
    from rich men's garments:
schappe not to be worn
    outside my master's shop. A kind
of peace, to bide my term & keep
    my countenance, drive
your kine to market, carry
    pails of grain to the chicken-run;
and then, when we at last convene
    our mutual hurt and pride, to feel
our hands slip unexpectedly together,
    our mouths seal promises, love's
brazen colour flush
    neck and breast, hearts fledge and flesh
hunger for bare flesh.

Suibne Plays Houseboy to the Hag of the Mill

Once
  my ear preferred
the rapt song of the blackbird
  to pillow talk. I wore
the feather-pelt & laughed:
  was not the cuckoo's plainsong sweeter
than the toll of wedding bells?
  Once
I was a fox in the field:
  I slept in ditches,
sossed milk from cow-blakes,
  far from the warm
and blether of women.
  Today, dismissed, I turn
to servitude without complaint.
  Pocketing your prayer book,
I find the pages lit
  with spoils from our last
battleground.
  Allow me to list
their vernacular names:
  Lady's Bedstraw,
Butcher's Broom,
  Maiden Pink.

Suibne Recalls His Freedom, and His Wife Éorann

                    Once
        I was a stag in the glen:
I saw the birch bathe queenly
        in a stream of heat
while I breakfasted on watercress,
        on vetch & oystergrass.
Once I was a grasshopper,
        finer than fishbones were the barbs on my bow,
then a grassblade, crowned
        with a diamond dewdrop.
Only when I ran
        from a shower of hailstones
to the appleblossom tree
        and saw hail fall
like brutal blossom
        (the blossom frail
as petals made of stone)
        did I think of Éorann:
the day we watched
        two squirrels mate;
magnolia petals falling
        around their mirrored question-mark.

Suibne Returns to Éorann but Finds Her Betrothed to G'uaire

It is seven years ago I cut
   a mistle thrush free
of a poem, declaring it
   too obvious
a symbol of unrest.
   Did I divine
how shortly you would boast
   a throstle's nest
high in the eaves
   of your true love's house?

Suibne in the Trees

When I hear the belling
    of the stag in the glen
my heart begins
    to pine and keen.

Acorns taste
    as sweet as ever
and I still savour
    the hazel's coffer,

but unmet lust
    and unseasoned grief
mar a man's life
    when his home is lost.

Silver birch, waltz
    in the wind that scatters
aspen leaves
    like staves in a battle.

Apple tree, apt
    to be looted by boys,
weather the storm
    with the rowan blossom.

Alder, shield me
    with your pallid branches.
Blackthorn, bless me
    with blood-dark sloes.

Ivy, hold yourself
    close as a halter.
Yew, stand to,
    at odds with the world.

Holly, be a shelter
    from the wind, a barrier.
Ash, be a spear-shaft
    hurled by a warrior.

Dearly it cost me
    to cross you, briar:
a scald of blood money,
    my palm in bloom.

Hateful to me
    as an evil word:
a rootless tree
    holding sway in the wood.

Suibne Recalls How He Came to be Cursed with the Flying Madness

When I heard
   how the otter's knuckled crown
had broken the lake water;
   and how the animal
most unnatural
   held a psalter in its jaw,
delivering the book
   immaculate
at the cleric's feet
   before turning tail
to melt back into its element,
   friend, I was perturbed.
Surely God meant
   Finn to be avenged
when He gave him the words: 'Suibne,
   my curse lights on you:
that you shall ever be ragged
   broken & naked
and your persecutor swift
   as the eagle in the heavens;
that you shall find
   death on a spear;
that peace & wisdom shall stand
   foreign to your sight
as they were the day
   of your great offence.'
May God forgive me.
   I was & am ever
for endless flight.

NOTES & DEDICATIONS

According to Culpeper (9)
The answer is honeysuckle.

Secret Papers (16)
See Tomas Tranströmer's 'Solitary Swedish Houses,' which includes the
lines 'they're burning / the forest's secret papers' (trs. Robin Fulton).

Blodeuwedd (19)
A 'jenny-houlet' is a Northumbrian name for a barn owl.

Gilgamesh Rebukes Ishtar (21)
Gilgamesh concerns the exploits of the warrior king Gilgamesh. His name
means 'Our ancestors were heroes' and he protected his people by killing
monsters such as Humbaba. At least, he protected his people when he
wasn't raping or killing them: Gilgamesh has a claim to being the first
tyrant, and the first war criminal. Ishtar, goddess of love and war, was
so impressed she tried to seduce our hero, who rejected her with this
speech (Tablet VI, lines 42-79). In his efficiency as a slayer of monsters,
Gilgamesh can be compared with later figures such as Beowulf and St
George. His arrogant rejection of the Female throws an interesting light
on the subtext of such myths; a Hughesian reading would be that the
rejection creates the monsters with which he fights. The oldest story in
the world readily finds contemporary resonances: Gilgamesh is king of
Uruk, in what is present-day Iraq.

To Photograph a Snow Crystal (28)
For Anna Woodford. Ukichiro Nakaya was the first person to grow a
snow crystal synthetically in a laboratory. At sub-zero temperatures, most
materials frost over, covering the individual snow crystals. Nakaya found
that the natural oils in rabbit hair prevented the nucleation of ice: he
could therefore suspend a snow crystal on a hair, and watch it develop.

The Permafrost: an A–Z (29)
Written while under the influence of the Magazine album *Secondhand
Daylight*.

Lebiyska Mova (32)
'Lebiyska Mova' is a secret language spoken by the Kobzari: itinerant
musicians of Ukraine. The Kobzari sang epic cycles of songs known as
'dumy', telling of Ukrainian history and the wars that formed the country.
A bandura is a lap harp with fifty five strings. The Kobzari had guilds,

designated territories, and an oral tradition thousands of years old. In other respects (such as their ambivalent social status as beggars/entertainers, and the fact that they were often blind) they were comparable with bluesmen such as Charlie Patton or Blind Willie McTell. The greatest Kobzari, Fedir, travelled where he liked. A misanthrope, Fedir slept in ditches between gigs and was nicknamed 'the Cold One'. In 1933, Stalin declared the Kobzari 'enemies of the people', and within a few years all but a handful disappeared.

Tristia (33)
In AD 8, Augustus Caesar relegated Publius Ovidius Naso to Tomis (now Constanza in Romania), officially because of the licentiousness of Ovid's *Ars Amatoria*. As this was published ten years earlier, it is unlikely to be the genuine reason. 'Relegation' (rather than 'exile') meant that Ovid retained his citizenship. This legal technicality had two major consequences: Ovid's wife would remain in Rome to look after his affairs, and a pardon from Augustus remained a possibility. So Ovid spent his time in Tomis writing *Tristia*: love poems to his wife, and poems of petition (aimed indirectly at Augustus) to be circulated around the capital. The plan did not succeed. These are loose versions of various poems from *Tristia* and *Epistulae Ex Ponto*.

Keening (48)
For Barry MacSweeney.

The Butcher's Daughter (49)
For William Oswald Young, 9th Northumberland Fusiliers/8th Royal Irish Hussars. Mia reckons Hitler was 'A man of the people', and asks 'Don't you remember how poor we were back then?' Her father says 'Mia is not a thief, it must be Hans.' In Dresden, the children ask for chocolate. Mia is reported as having said 'When Bill comes, give these to him please.'

Suibne Changed (55-62)
Suibne Geilt is a series of poems dating from 9th-century Ireland. In the 12th century, further poems and a prose narrative were added and the result called *Buile Suibne*. The poems tell the story of King Suibne, who insulted the cleric Rónán Finn (later St Ronan) and was consequently transformed into a bird. With a bird's fearfulness, Suibne travelled around Ireland, avoiding human contact (even that of his friend Loingsechán and his wife Éorann), sometimes pursued by the Hag of the Mill. The story finds parallels in the Welsh folktales concerning Myrddin Wyllt (Mad Merlin). 'Suibne in the Trees' is fairly faithful to one of the 12th-century additions; elsewhere I have translated and invented freely.